a study of
Ephesians

Live Out Your Identity in Christ

SHANTÉ GROSSETT

A Study of Ephesians: Live Out Your Identity in Christ

Table of Contents

a quick note before you dive in

I am so grateful that you have decided to join me in studying the book of Ephesians for the next few weeks! I believe that all Christians need to understand the message, purpose, and application of Ephesians.

Ephesians communicates the foundational truths of the gospel, how it informs our identity in Christ and then teaches us how to live an empowered Christian life in light of those truths. God is calling us to be more than just Christians in name. Our entire lives should be transformed by the gospel of Jesus Christ.

I learned so much putting this study together. The Holy Spirit really spoke to my heart and preached this message to me even before allowing me to share it with anyone else.

This is why I'm so confident about this study. I know that if you allow the Holy Spirit to lead you as you study, you will walk away having gained a whole lot.

The study is very interactive so be prepared to have your pen and highlighter in hand and a Bible in front of you. We will be covering a lot but don't worry, the content is divided into sessions that should take you approximately twenty to thirty minutes per day.

Of course, you are free to go at your own pace and work through the study more quickly or more slowly as you see fit.

Again, I'm so excited that you're joining me for this study and I pray that it's a huge blessing to you!

With love,
Shanté

Before you get started, I have a few suggestions:

- I highly encourage you to print out this study and put it in a binder or folder. It will be so much easier to follow along with a printed version.

- Read each passage at least twice. When you read it the first time, make no observations. Just simply read and try to comprehend what it's saying. Read the passage again a second time and make note of anything that stands out to you. Don't worry too much about what to write down during the second reading because I'll guide you through it. As you complete more of the study, you should become more comfortable writing down your own observations in addition to the ones I point out for you.

- When reading the passage, look out for repetition, transitional words, names, places, dates, and words to define. Paying close attention to each of these will help you as you interpret what you are reading.

- Asking yourself who, what, when, where, and why can also be very helpful as you begin to dissect each passage and try to understand what it's saying.

- Always start and end your Bible study time with prayer. Remember, the Holy Spirit is your teacher and if you simply ask him to help you understand the word, he will.

- I encourage you to go beyond this study! Draw your own conclusions, ask your own questions, and think of your own applications in addition to the ones here.

- I have more resources on how to study the Bible on my website. If you're brand new to Bible study, I encourage you to take some time to check out those resources as well.

- Finally, I love seeing your journey through the study. Feel free to share your photos on social media and tag me @herstyleoftea for a chance to be featured!

Are you ready? Let's dive in!

The Ultimate Blessing

IN HIM WE HAVE REDEMPTION THROUGH HIS BLOOD, THE FORGIVENESS OF OUR TRESPASSES, ACCORDING TO THE RICHES OF HIS GRACE, *ephesians 1:7*

Day 1: Intro to Ephesians

Today, we will look at some important details about the book of Ephesians. When starting any new book in the Bible, you should always try to learn about its author, historical context, the type of writing, the audience, and its intended message. Understanding these key details will be beneficial as you begin to read, interpret, and apply the text.

The letter to the Ephesians was written by the Apostle Paul in AD 62 while he was imprisoned in Rome.

Read Acts 22:3,28, Philippians 3:5, Acts 7:54-60, Acts 9:1-19, Acts 15:1-29, Acts 16:16-25, Acts 21:10-14, Acts 21:26-36 to learn more about the life and ministry of Paul

Where was Paul born?

_____

List three keywords that describes Paul's identity (See Acts 22:3,28 & Philippians 3:5)

_____

_____

_____

What happened to Paul at Damascus? Describe the events briefly.

_____

_____

_____

_____

_____

_____

Why were Paul and Silas arrested?

_____

_____

_____

Who prophesied that Paul would be bound in Jerusalem?

_____

Where did a mob try to kill Paul?

_____

It's clear that the Apostle Paul was very influential in spreading Christianity among the ancient world. He traveled on four missionary journeys where he planted churches and preached the gospel. We see that he also wrote many letters to various churches and its leaders. Paul wrote at least thirteen books in the New Testament. It's amazing how a man who previously persecuted the church became one its most prominent leaders.

Look at the timeline below to get an idea of the timing between Paul's conversion, his missionary journey to Ephesus, and the writing of the letter to the Ephesians.

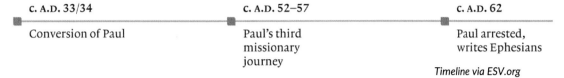

c. A.D. 33/34	c. A.D. 52–57	c. A.D. 62
Conversion of Paul	Paul's third missionary journey	Paul arrested, writes Ephesians

Timeline via ESV.org

Ephesians is unique because it doesn't address a specific problem like many of Paul's other letters did. Many believe that it was a circular letter meant for the Ephesians and other churches in the surrounding regions. It communicated Christian doctrine and morals to a new and growing church. Paul also wrote letters to the Colossians and to Philemon during this time.

The City of Ephesus

Ephesus was a wealthy port city in the Roman province of Asia. It was a very important city since it was a central trading point in the Mediterranean region. Think of New York City or Washington D.C.

Like in many other Gentile cities, the Ephesians worshipped false gods and goddesses. Their primary goddess was Artemis and her temple is actually one of the seven wonders of the world. Artemis was worshiped by many around the ancient world at the time. Ephesus was the center of this worship and devoted many eunuch priests, virgin priestesses, and religious prostitutes for her worship. Many of the rituals involved severe sexual immorality.

The Ephesians most likely heard the gospel preached by Priscilla and Aquila. After his second missionary journey, Paul left them there to continue the work of the ministry (See Acts 18:18,19,26). Paul went back to Ephesus and officially established the church during his third missionary journey. He remained there for three years and then left Timothy to oversee the church. Paul was concerned about influential leaders who were preaching false teachings. Timothy was responsible for guarding the Ephesians from these quick spreading lies.

In Acts 19, we see that many people earned their living from creating shrines to Artemis. When Paul came to Ephesus preaching the gospel, their livelihood was threatened since many people were turning away from idolatry to worshipping the Lord.

Map via biblestudy.org

Read Acts 18:18-28, Acts 19

Who were Priscilla and Aquila?

_____

_____

_____

_____

Where was Apollos from?

_____

_____

How did Priscilla and Aquila help Apollos?

_____

_____

_____

_____

How long was Paul in the synagogue preaching about the kingdom of God?

_____

_____

List some of the miracles God did through Paul.

_____

_____

_____

_____

_____

What was the name of the man who started the riot against Paul in Ephesus?

_____

_____

Why were he and his followers angry with Paul?

_____

_____

How did the rioting end? What did the town clerk speak up and say?

_____

_____

_____

_____

Well, it's clear that lots of important things happened at Ephesus. Preaching, miracles, and even riots. There was a lot at stake in Ephesus. It was an important city and the gospel could travel far and wide through it.

Message of Ephesians

Ephesians can be divided into two sections. The first half deals with the believer's Christian identity and inheritance in Christ. In light of the truths established in the first half, Paul instructs believers how to live out the Christian life in the second half.

Key themes

- Without God, all people are spiritually dead and influenced by Satan
- God has called his people to redemption and holiness in Christ
- God's mercy and grace saves sinners. We receive this gift by faith in Christ.
- Jesus' sacrifice on the cross unites all people into one body as a new creation
- As Christians, we are called to live holy and righteous lives
- Holiness includes submitting to proper authorities, in home and family life, and those in authority must love and care for those submitted to them
- Jesus gave the church important gifts to promote unity, maturity, and strength against the enemy and his plans

Themes paraphrased via ESV.org

Pause & Reflect

Did you learn anything new about the life of Paul or the city of Ephesus today?

_____

_____

_____

_____

What do you hope to learn from studying Ephesians for the next few weeks?

_____

_____

_____

_____

Write out a short prayer to God asking him for help to understand the scripture and wisdom to apply it in your life.

_____

_____

_____

_____

Day 2: Spiritual Blessings

Read Ephesians 1:1-19

In your own words, what is this passage saying?

_____

_____

_____

_____

_____

_____

_____

_____

_____

_____

_____

_____

_____

_____

_____

_____

_____

_____

_____

Here are a few important points you should take away from this passage:

- God gave us spiritual blessings through Christ
- We are now adopted children of God and our inheritance has been sealed by the Holy Spirit.
- Paul gives thanks for the Ephesians (and us!). He prays that God would give them wisdom and knowledge to understand the wonderful blessing they have in Christ.
- Finally, Paul speaks of how Jesus is seated at the right hand of the Father and has all power.

blessings
on blessings
on blessings
on blessings

What are some of the things you have been blessed with here on earth? List them below.

_____

_____

_____

_____

_____

Fill in the blank.

God has blessed us in Christ with _____ spiritual blessings in the heavenly places.

I want you to really think about this. God has given us *every* spiritual blessing. We don't lack anything at all. I don't know about you but that gives me chills.

Do you ever feel like you're not enough? I know I do sometimes. But this is a beautiful reminder that we have everything we need in Christ. His sufficiency is far greater than our deficiencies.

Why are spiritual blessings so significant?

Okay, so we just spoke about how awesome these spiritual blessings are and I even told you it gives me chills. But, why? Why is this so important?

Well, our spiritual blessings are what gives us access into the heavenly places. *Okay, so what?*

Read Revelation 21:9-27

This is a picture of the beauty of our inheritance in Christ. I mean, streets of pure gold? Pearl gates? Now, I know this city is beautiful. But, let's take it a step further. This city was created by God for his people. The beauty of this city points to the splendor of God.

Our spiritual blessings in Christ give us access to God. We're going to talk about this access later but I just want you to take a second to think about that. God has given us the greatest blessing there is. You and I can name some things we've been blessed with, as well as some things we would like to be blessed with here on earth. But the spiritual blessings we have in Christ far outweigh every other blessing we could think of.

And the twelve gates were twelve pearls, each of the gates made of a single pearl, and the street of the city was pure gold, like transparent glass.

Revelation 21:21 ESV

11

You were chosen <u>before</u> the foundation of the world.

Read verses 4-5

God chose us before the foundation of the world so that we could do what?

_____

Remember High School P.E.? I don't know about you, but I was always the *last* to be chosen. I don't have an athletic bone in my body. When I did get chosen, it was because the captain of the team had no other option left. And rightfully so because I wasn't doing their team much justice.

Look at the wording of this phrase. God chose us before the foundation of the world. He didn't randomly choose you because you were the last person left. Long before you were born, he predestined you to become his daughter.

As his daughter, he has called you to be both **holy** and **blameless** before him. So, what does that mean?

HOLY	BLAMELESS
this refers to our moral purity	this speaks to our freedom from the guilt of past sin

Read Jude 1:24-25, Colossians 1:21-22, and 1 Thessalonians 3:11-13

God is able to keep us from doing what?

_____

_____

Who has reconciled us into his body by his death?

_____

_____

Who establishes our hearts blameless in holiness?

_____

_____

Taken together, what do you learn from these passages?

_____

_____

_____

We don't make ourselves holy & blameless, God does.

We don't make ourselves holy and blameless. God makes us this way. If we had to do this on our own, we'd never succeed. Instead, God works in us to make us both holy and blameless.

Pause & Reflect

God did something really amazing for us when he gave us this spiritual blessing. But, why did he do this? Take a second to think about that.

Verse 5 tells us that God did this for us according to the purpose of his will for his glory. We'll get into this later but I want you to realize that it wasn't because we were good or worthy of this. This depended on God's goodness, not ours.

Day 3: God's plan for us and the world

Read verses 7-10

God plans to redeem, forgive, and unite all things in him.

Let's dive into each of these further.

Redemption

The Greek word used here is *apolytrosis*. It means to redeem someone or something by paying a price, to let one go free upon receiving the price, or to release a captive by the paying of a ransom.

God redeemed us by the shedding of the blood of Christ.

Up until Jesus' death, people were separated from God. Only Jews, a small group of people chosen by God, had any form of fellowship with him. But even their fellowship lacked something.

All humans owed God a debt because of our sin. Unfortunately, we couldn't pay our debt. Jesus stepped into our place and paid the price owed. He redeemed us from the bondage of sin, setting us free.

See 1 Peter 2:24, Romans 3:24, and 1 Peter 1:18-19

Forgiveness

God didn't just redeem us from sin, he also forgave our trespasses. He no longer holds our sin against us. Our standing with Christ is as if we have never sinned.

See Hebrews 9:22, 1 John 2:12, and Matthew 26:28

Unity

Finally, God plans to unite all things in Christ. We are united with each other and with God.

Unity and uniformity are not the same thing.

Grab a dictionary (or google!)

Define unity:

_____
_____
_____

Define uniformity:

_____
_____
_____

Read 1 Corinthians 12:12-31

Paul uses the physical body to illustrate how the spiritual body of Christ works. Within our bodies, there are many organs but we are still one body. Each part of the body is different but work together to keep the body alive. This is how we function as members of the body of Christ.

Uniformity would be a **huge** problem within the body of Christ. Imagine a body made up of all eyes or all hands! Weird, right?

Uniformity renders the body useless but unity makes us strong.

Later, we'll talk about how diversity within the body of Christ actually promotes unity beautifully.

God plans to unite all things in Christ

Day 4: Predestined for an inheritance

Read verses 11-14

If you feel comfortable, grab a pen or highlighter and circle "inheritance" and "predestined" in your Bible. Now, underline "purpose of him who works all things according to the counsel of his will." It's always great to highlight or circle anything that stands out as you read so you can look into it further later.

Read John 15:16, Acts 13:48, and Romans 8:28-30

What do you learn from these passages?

_____

_____

_____

_____

_____

God has predestined us for salvation. This is our inheritance. We touched on this before but God didn't randomly decide to save us one day. He predestined, or pre-planned, this long before the world was made.

What do you learn about God's character from these verses?

_____

_____

_____

_____

_____

According to Ligonier Ministries predestination shows the glory of God in five ways. I want to point out three. It shows the unchangeable character of God, God's commitment to his eternal purposes, and the beauty of God's grace.

He didn't have to choose us but he did. Isn't such a comfort to know that God is committed to his plans towards us and it doesn't depend on us?

Read Genesis 12:1-3, Deuteronomy 7:6-8, and Psalm 135:4

God also chose Israel out of all the other nations surrounding them. Deuteronomy 7 tells us that God didn't choose them because they were a great and awesome nation. He chose them because he wanted to.

Likewise, God has also chosen each of us who have received the Gospel to become his sons and daughters.

Now, predestination doesn't mean that God forces our hand and makes us saved. No, he gives us free will. But, at the same time, he knows and has already predetermined that we would choose him too.

The Holy Spirit as our down-payment

Let's look at verses 13 and 14 more closely.

What do you think it means?

_____

_____

_____

_____

_____

Has there ever been a time in your life where you've felt too far gone for God to still love you? What was it like?

_____

_____

_____

_____

I wanted to cry tears of joy when I read this. The greek word for "guarantee" in this passage relates more closely to our English word "down payment."

I'm going to try to explain this with an analogy. Are you familiar with the process of buying a house? If you aren't, before you can purchase a house, you have to make a down payment. Now, once you make that down payment, the house is practically yours. Of course, you can go back and say that you no longer want to purchase the house. But other than that, no one can take the house away from you. It's yours.

You and I are the house and God is the buyer. The Holy Spirit is his down payment. One day, he will receive us and we will dwell with him forever. But until then, the Holy Spirit within us is the sign that we belong to God. We are sealed with the Spirit and our Heavenly Father does not take his seal away from us. Isn't that good news?!

I don't know about you but I have failed so many times. I've done things I shouldn't have as a believer. But, God has never said, "You know what, forget about that one. She's messed up too many times." No, you and I are *sealed*. God promises to complete the work he has begun in us.

God will complete the work *he has begun in us.*

How does it feel to know that God has never and will never leave you?

_____

_____

_____

_____

Day 5: Thanksgiving & Prayer

Read verses 15-22

Why was Paul giving thanks for the Ephesian church?

_____

_____

_____

_____

_____

What is Paul praying for God to give them?

_____

_____

_____

_____

_____

Why do you think it was important for the Ephesians to experience these things from God?

_____

_____

_____

_____

_____

Who is receiving the "glorious inheritance in the saints"?

_____

_____

_____

_____

_____

Paul gives thanks for the Ephesians because of their faith in Jesus and their love for each other. He also prays for them continuously that God would give them wisdom to understand the hope and calling they have in Christ.

At first glance, you may think that Paul is speaking about our inheritance. But he isn't. He's speaking about Jesus receiving us as his inheritance. Isn't that amazing? God sees his people as precious in his sight. He has done so much to have us as his own.

Read Isaiah 43:1-7

This passage gives us some more insight into the lengths God will go for his people. He is with us to the end.

Based on this passage, do you know why God goes to these kinds of lengths for his people?

_____

_____

_____

_____

_____

He does this because he made us for his glory and we are called by his name. This is why even though we turned away from God into sin, he still calls us home. He made us for a specific purpose and it is his desire that we live out that purpose.

Paul introduces some really incredible things in this opening chapter, and he will elaborate on them throughout the rest of this letter. But, the thing is, we need the Spirit to help us understand all of this. No matter how many eloquent words Paul uses to describe this wonderful truth, we can't fully grasp it unless it is revealed by the Spirit.

This also applies for any passage you study in the Bible. Before you begin, always pray and ask God to open your eyes to understand his word. Then approach it expectantly, waiting for him to teach you.

So just as Paul prayed for the Ephesians, I'm praying for you too. May God open your eyes to understand the weight of this glorious message.

Read verses 20-23

Who is seated far above all rule, authority, power, and dominion?

_____

_____

_____

_____

_____

Fill in the blank.

And he put _____ under his feet and gave him as _____ to the church, which is his _____, the _____ of him who fills all in all.

The same power that God uses to open our eyes to the truth of the gospel is the power that he worked in Christ to:

- Raise him from the dead
- Seat him in heavenly places
- Exalt him above rulers, authority, powers, and dominion
- Exalt him above every name that we could possibly think of
- Allow him to reign not just now but forever

This is a pretty big deal.

Would you consider yourself to have strong faith in Jesus like the Ephesians did? Why or why not?

_____

_____

_____

If you answered no, what do you think is holding you back from this kind of faith?

_____

_____

_____

Could someone give thanks to God for the way you love others?

_____

_____

_____

If not, how can you improve?

_____

_____

_____

Paul prayed that the Ephesians would understand the gospel. Is there anyone in your life who needs to understand the gospel? Take some time to pray for them.

_____

_____

_____

_____

_____

_____

_____

_____

_____

_____

_____

_____

_____

_____

_____

Grace, Grace, and More Grace

FOR IT IS BY GRACE YOU HAVE BEEN SAVED, THROUGH FAITH – AND THIS IS NOT FROM YOURSELVES, IT IS THE GIFT OF GOD *ephesians 2:8*

Day 1: Dead in trespasses and sin

Read Ephesians 2:1-22

Before we get started, let's define some key words. Grab a dictionary and look up each of these words.

Trespasses

Sin

Grace

Gentile

Jew

Circumcision

Ordinance

Citizen

Saint

Summarize chapter two in your own words.

_____
_____
_____
_____
_____
_____
_____
_____
_____
_____
_____
_____
_____
_____
_____
_____
_____
_____
_____
_____
_____
_____
_____

Paul speaks about the reality of our sinful state without Christ. We were dead in our trespasses and sins and lived a worldly lifestyle, following the influence of the devil. But, the good news is, Jesus made us alive by saving us through his grace. We are now seated in heavenly places in Christ. We must remember that this gift of God we have now received is by grace and not our works. Not only were we separated from God, we were also separated from his people, Israel. There was hostility between God's people and the gentiles. But now that wall has been broken down through Christ and we are reconciled to each other. We are all one in Christ and share in the inheritance of Christ.

Read verses 1-3

We just finished studying spiritual blessings and now we're talking about death. What? Well, remember how Paul prayed that the Ephesians would understand the greatness of their inheritance in Christ? In order to understand the weight of the good news, we must also understand the weight of the bad news. This is why we need to talk about death.

Paul says that we were dead in trespasses and sins. How did we get this way?

Read Genesis 2:17 and Genesis 3

What did God say would happen if they ate from the tree of the knowledge of good and evil?

_____

_____

_____

What did the serpent say to Eve to get her to doubt?

_____

_____

_____

_____

What did Adam and Eve do when they heard God walking in the garden?

_____

_____

_____

True or false. God drove Adam and Eve out of the garden.

In Genesis 3, we see that Adam and Eve disobeyed God, ate of the tree, and died a spiritual death.

In your own words, what is spiritual death?

_____

_____

_____

Spiritual death is separation from God.

Read Romans 5:12-14

Death literally *reigned*. It reigned over all of us and we had no escape.

Okay, so what's the big deal? Why does it matter if we're separated from God?

- We're separated from our true identity
- We live a purposeless life less than what God intended for us
- We start to produce symptoms of separation from God. Namely, sin.

Finally, separation from God leads to eternal damnation. It's a scary thing but it's the reality for those apart from Christ.

> separation from God leads to eternal damnation.

The Sinful Nature

This is a bit of a trick question but if you can remember back to your childhood, who taught you how to sin?

_____

_____

_____

_____

_____

No one, right? This is because we were born with a sinful nature. We have a natural disposition towards sin.

Read Psalm 51:5

According to verses 2 and 3, What are some of the things we used to do because of our sin?

_____

_____

_____

_____

_____

_____

_____

_____

_____

_____

Essentially, we followed the course of the world, followed the prince of the power of the air (who is Satan), and finally, we did whatever we desired. We had no restraint. Our sin made us eligible for the wrath of God.

Pause & Reflect

Do you believe the words you just read? Do you believe that you were deserving of the wrath of God? If you don't believe this yet, it's okay. Pray and ask God to open your eyes and heart to receive the truth. If you do believe this, great. It's foundational for what we will discuss next.

Day 2: The grace that is greater than our sin

Read verses 4-7

Grab your Bible and circle or underline "but God." Circle or underline anything else that stood out to you as you read this section.

"But" is an important word here because it signifies an important contrast between our past and what God has done for us to ensure our future. The good news of the gospel is so much beautiful when we understand the severity of the bad news. When we can understand the weight of our sin, we can also recognize the glory of God's grace.

Unfortunately, many churches preach half of the gospel. They preach that Jesus died to save us and that's true. But, what did Jesus die to save us from? What did he save us for? The gospel isn't for "okay" people who made a few mistakes. *(spoiler alert: there are none)* The gospel is for dead people who need to be made alive.

Take a second to reflect on your "but God" moment. What was life like before you came to know Jesus? How has he transformed you?

_____
_____
_____
_____
_____
_____
_____
_____
_____
_____

As you begin walking with Jesus, he starts to transform your life from the inside out. It's a process and none of us are at the same place on this journey. But there should be transformation that continues to happen as each day goes by. If you're uncertain about whether or not this process is happening in your life, ask yourself these questions:

Have I begun loving God more? Have I started to hate sin more? Do I delight in God's word more? Do I feel greater conviction towards the sins I once loved?

If you answered "yes" to these questions, chances are you are growing as a believer. That's great news!

But God, being rich in mercy, because of the great love with which he loved us ...

Ephesians 2:4 ESV

So, back to your "but God" moment. This was God's plan from the beginning. When Adam and Eve sinned, it looked like there was no hope left for the world. But even then, God had a plan to restore the earth.

What challenges are you currently facing? How can you recognize God's hand turning those challenges around for good?

_____

_____

_____

_____

_____

God was rich in what towards us?

He was rich in mercy towards us. He saved us because of his love for us.

Here Paul makes it clear that we are saved by grace. Even though we were dead in sin, God made us alive. God didn't choose us because we were good or even "almost" good. He didn't save us because we started trying harder. He saved us despite the fact that we were still dead in trespasses and sin.

C.S Lewis said something really profound and I want to paraphrase it for you:

Jesus didn't come to make bad people good. He came to make dead people alive.

God performed the greatest miracle known to mankind when Jesus died on the cross. This miracle allowed billions of people who were dead to rise up and walk into new life.

Salvation isn't something to take lightly. I mean, have you ever seen a dead person come to life? Probably not, right? That would be a miracle. Our salvation is a miracle.

Take a look at verse 6 again.

> Fill in the blank.
>
> God raised us up with him and _____ us with him in the _____ in _____.

Just as Jesus died and was raised from the dead, we were dead and raised to life. Just as Jesus is seated at the right hand of the Father, we are seated with Christ in the heavenly places.

While we're not physically seated in heavenly places right now, we are spiritually.

What do you think it means to be seated in heavenly places?

_____

_____

_____

_____

_____

This means that we are citizens of heaven. We still live on this earth but our minds and hearts are set on God and his kingdom instead of the things of the world.

Read Colossians 3:1 and 1 Peter 2:11-12

According to these verses, how should we live our lives?

_____

_____

_____

_____

_____

Since our citizenship is in heaven, we are now strangers in this world. We no longer live like the world does because we are not like the world. As citizens of heaven, it's our duty to conduct ourselves as such. Christ secured our new identity as children of God but it is our responsibility to walk it out.

What is your biggest struggle when it comes to living out your Christian identity?

_____

_____

_____

_____

_____

The beautiful thing about our walk with Christ is that Jesus walks with us. He doesn't leave us to fend for ourselves. He has given us his Spirit and his word to help us live godly lives. Later on in this study, we will discuss some practical ways to live out our Christian identity.

Immeasurable riches of his grace

Read Ephesians 2:7 again and read Romans 5:20-21

There's a beautiful hymn that I love so much. It's called *Grace Greater*. Take a second and read the chorus of the hymn.

> *Grace, grace, God's grace, grace that will pardon and cleanse within; grace, grace, God's grace, grace*
> *that is greater than all our sin.*

Notice the language in this verse. God wants to show us the immeasurable riches of his grace. The grace that we've received from people in our lives is nothing compared to the grace of God. The riches of God's grace is *immeasurable*. God has poured out, is pouring out, and will continue to pour out his grace on us.

You think your sin is great? God's grace is greater. The worst sin in the world is no match for the immeasurable riches of God's grace.

What have you been taught in the past about good works, grace, and salvation? Is it consistent with what you know now?

_____
_____
_____
_____
_____
_____
_____
_____
_____

Has anyone ever shown you grace? What was it like?

_____
_____
_____
_____
_____
_____
_____
_____
_____

Why do you think it matters that Jesus came to make dead people alive instead of bad people good?

_____
_____
_____
_____

Is there anything from this section you still don't understand or want to study further? Write them down here.

_____
_____
_____
_____
_____

Let's close out this section with prayer. Share your thoughts, needs, questions, and concerns with God.

_____
_____
_____
_____

Day 3: Not a result of works

Read Ephesians 2:8-10

The phrase "for by grace you have been saved" has been repeated here. Repetition in scripture signifies importance. Paul wants us to know that this incredible inheritance is a gift of God's grace, not something we can earn.

Yet, we do play a role here. Faith is how we respond to God's grace. God gives us free will and if we don't receive his gift, he won't force us to be saved.

Blake Guichet of the Crappy Christian Co, said these words once, and they ring true: "The ground is even at the foot of the cross." We can't boast in our salvation because it was a gift God gave us while we were still sinners.

If we're being honest, sometimes we are guilty of attempting to boast in our salvation. For example, we may boast about how long we've been saved, how much scripture we know by heart, how great we are at Bible study, how eloquently we pray... but all of this boasting is in vain.

If we really want to boast, here's what we should be boasting in: **the cross of Christ.**

> *But far be it from me to boast except in the cross of our Lord Jesus Christ, by which the world has been crucified to me, and I to the world. Galatians 6:14 (ESV)*

The oxford dictionary says that boasting is talking with excessive pride and self-satisfaction about one's achievements. Please understand that there's nothing wrong with celebrating your achievements and sharing it with others. However, boasting goes beyond merely celebrating and becomes overly self-focused.

Why do we boast?

John Piper tells us that boasting is the outward form of the inner condition of pride.

- We boast to try and exalt ourselves. In other words, we try to make ourselves look better. But the one we should be exalting is God and when we boast, we attempt to take his glory.
- We boast for validation. But we must remember that we have already been validated by God, not because of what we did, but because of what Jesus did.

God's masterpiece

Have you ever created something you were incredibly proud of? Describe how you felt about it.

_____

_____

_____

_____

_____

_____

The last verse of this section tells us that we are God's workmanship. In other words, we are God's masterpiece. He created us to do good works that glorify him. While our works do not save us, we should be producing spirit-led works by the grace of God. Works can be the evidence of our salvation but they are not the cause of our salvation.

We are saved by grace and grace alone. It was a beautiful gift that God gave us when Jesus died on the cross. We can't boast in salvation because we never earned it to begin with. It was simply given to us.

Pause & Reflect

What does it mean to you to know that we can't earn our salvation?

_____
_____
_____
_____
_____

Think over the past week. Did you boast about anything in your heart or out loud? If so, what was it?

_____
_____
_____
_____
_____

Take a few minutes to pray and ask God to help you live in light of the truth that we don't earn our salvation. If you struggle with boasting in your works, ask God to help you remember that all the gifts you have come from him.

_____
_____
_____
_____
_____
_____
_____
_____
_____
_____
_____
_____
_____
_____
_____

Day 4: Alienation

Read Ephesians 3:11-13 and Genesis 17:1-14

Not only were we as Gentile believers dead in trespasses and sin, we were also alienated from Israel, God's people.

Gentiles were known as the **uncircumcision**.

According to Genesis 17:1-14, why were Jewish men circumcised?

_____
_____
_____
_____
_____

What was the covenant between God and Abraham?

_____
_____
_____
_____
_____

God told Abraham that if he walked **blamelessly** before God, he would make him the father of many nations and his offspring would be blessed.

Let's do some critical thinking. How do you think uncircumcised males were seen within this community?

_____
_____
_____
_____
_____

Uncircumcised males and their families did not share in the Abrahamic covenant and were not a part of the family of nations God would bless.

This is why Paul says the Ephesians were "strangers to the covenant of promise" and had "no hope and without God in the world."

We were on our own. But the good news is that the blood of Christ has brought us near.

Jesus established a new covenant when he died. Now, all people who call on the name of the Lord can be saved. (See Romans 10:13) We now have hope and instead of being far from the family of God, we are now welcomed into it.

Read verses 14-18

Remember how I mentioned that the Gentiles were separated from Israel? Well, they weren't just separated. There was hostility and tension between the two groups. When Jesus died on the cross, he broke down the source of the hostility so that the two could become united.

Wait a minute? Doesn't the Bible say Jesus didn't abolish the law?

Read Matthew 5:17-20

The word "abolished" appears in both Matthew 5:17-20 and Ephesians 2:14-18. But in the original greek text, they have different meanings. Let's look at them:

Katalusai - to destroy, overthrow   Katargesas - to render inoperative

Let's rewrite Ephesians 2:15 with the greek words:

> For he himself is our peace, who has made us both one and has broken down in his flesh the dividing wall of hostility by **rendering** the law of commandments expressed in ordinances **inoperative**, that he might create in himself one new man in place of the two, so making peace,

The law of commandments expressed in ordinances became inoperative to keep the Gentiles outside of the promise. Jesus did not abolish the law, he actually fulfilled it so that the law is written now on our hearts:

For this is the covenant that I will make with the house of Israel after those days, declares the LORD: I will put my law within them, and I will write it on their hearts. And I will be their God, and they shall be my people. Jeremiah 31:33

However, Jesus abolished its power to keep the Gentiles out.

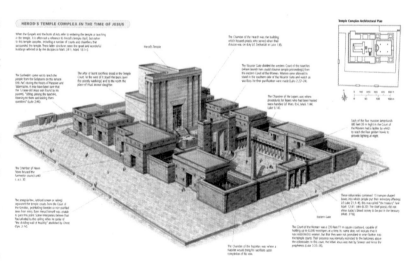

Map via Ingodsimage.com

Interestingly enough, there was a literal wall of hostility. During the reign of Herod the Great, there was a courtyard around the temple designated for gentiles. There was an inscription on the outer wall letting them know that if they did pass the courtyard, they would be risking their lives.

Pause & Reflect

Why do you think it's important that there is no hostility between members of the body of Christ?

_____
_____
_____
_____
_____

Do you ever feel like your past makes you less of a Christian than other people? What truth can you stand on from this passage to combat those feelings?

_____
_____
_____
_____
_____
_____
_____
_____
_____
_____

The gentiles were literally alienated from Jewish life, culture, and worship. Have you ever felt alienated from a group of people you wanted to belong to? What was it like?

_____
_____
_____
_____
_____
_____
_____
_____
_____
_____

For he himself is our peace, who has made us both one and has broken down in his flesh the dividing wall of hostility

Ephesians 2:14

Day 5: One instead of two

Read Ephesians 2:17-22

Now all people who believe in Jesus are one. God has reconciled both groups to himself through the cross.

Read Luke 15:11-24 and write down the key points.

_____
_____
_____
_____
_____
_____
_____
_____
_____
_____

Both sons needed the Father's love. Both had things in their heart that were not okay.

Jesus preached peace to those who were *near* and to those who were *far*. All people need Jesus.

Whether you grew up in a Christian background or not, you still need Jesus and the Gospel. Salvation is given only to those who believe by faith. You may know all the church songs, Bible stories, and even be fluent in Christianese but if you have not repented of your sin and surrendered your life to Jesus, you need to do that. This is the only way to receive the inheritance of God.

Write out verses 20 and 22

Verse 20:

Verse 22:

We have an assurance that we are no longer outsiders to the promises of God. We are members of his family. This family is the most important one there is. Think about the foundation it's built on. Apostles and prophets and Jesus is the cornerstone (that holds together) this foundation. Finally, God is building all of us together into a place for him to dwell by the Spirit. This is God's grace-filled plan for the world. Adam and Eve sinned in the beginning but even then God had a glorious plan. Isn't that amazing?

Pause & Reflect

We did a shorter study today.

So, for the rest of your quiet time, reflect on what you have learned from this chapter so far. Take this space below to journal about any of the themes that stood out to you. Was there anything surprising? Were you moved by anything? Was anything hard to believe?

Present all of your thoughts, questions, and concerns before God in writing.

Don't be afraid to be honest with God. He knows your heart and he simply wants to hear from you.

week 3

The glorious gospel & our identity in Christ

NOW TO HIM WHO IS ABLE TO DO FAR MORE ABUNDANTLY THAN ALL THAT WE ASK OR THINK, ACCORDING TO THE POWER AT WORK WITHIN US,

ephesians 3:20

Day 1: Suffering for Christ's Sake

Read Ephesians 3:1-20

How does Paul describe himself according to verse 1?

_____
_____
_____
_____
_____
_____
_____

What mystery was made known to Paul by revelation? (This was also revealed to Peter in Acts 10)

_____
_____
_____
_____
_____
_____
_____

Paul describes himself as the least of whom?

_____
_____
_____
_____
_____
_____

What does Paul pray that the body of believers receive?

_____
_____
_____
_____
_____
_____

Write out verses 20 and 21.

Verse 20:

Verse 21:

Suffering for Christ's sake

Read verses 1-6

Paul describes himself as a prisoner of Christ here. It makes sense because he was literally writing this letter from a Roman prison and he was put in prison for preaching the gospel. Let's look at some historical context for this.

Read Acts 20:22-27

If you were going on a trip and you heard that there was potential danger there, would you still go? Why or why not?

_____
_____
_____
_____
_____
_____
_____

I'll be honest, I probably wouldn't go. But Paul went to Jerusalem knowing that he might be harmed there. The message of the gospel was so important that Paul was willing to risk his physical safety. He was truly willing to suffer for the name of Christ.

He knew how important the gospel really was. The gospel was and is revolutionary.

For further reading: the entire account of how Paul ended up imprisoned in Rome spans from Acts 20-27.

Paul was willing to identify both with the glory that came from being a child of God as well as the hardships. We can't just claim our identity in Christ when it will produce good for us. We must also be willing to claim it when it involves suffering.

Let's look at some passages about suffering.

Read 2 Timothy 2:3, Romans 5:3-5, 1 Peter 4:12-19

How much does the gospel mean to you? Are you willing to walk through hardships for the sake of Christ?

_____
_____
_____
_____
_____
_____
_____

The truth is, we will suffer for Christ. The good news is that Christ doesn't leave us alone to suffer with no hope. He's with us and he gives us strength to endure what we're faced with.

What hardships are you facing in this season of your life?

_____
_____
_____
_____
_____
_____
_____

What does Paul's response to suffering teach you about how you should respond to your hardships?

_____
_____
_____
_____
_____
_____
_____

Suffering for Christ isn't fun. But, what are some of the good things that can come from this kind of suffering?

_____
_____
_____
_____
_____
_____

Take a moment to pray and ask God to give you strength to endure hardships and suffering.

_____
_____

_____
_____
_____
_____
_____

Least of all the saints

Read verses 7-13

Why do you think Paul referred to himself as the least of all the saints?

_____
_____
_____
_____
_____
_____
_____

Paul may have referred to himself this way because of his former life as a persecutor of Christians. We know Paul was once spiritually blind. When he encountered Jesus at Damascus, his eyes were opened. So, God used a previously blind man to open the eyes of many who were also blind so that they could see.

All of this was only by the grace of God.

Do you ever feel unworthy to show up and do the things God is calling you to do? Describe your experience.

_____
_____
_____
_____
_____
_____

Remember that like Paul, God has given you grace to do what he's calling you to. This doesn't mean it will be easy but you'll have the strength to do it. Your past doesn't disqualify you. In fact, God often uses our past struggles as the launching point of our current ministry.

I absolutely love this quote.

> *Your ministry is found where you've been broken. Your testimony is found where you've been restored.*

Consider that maybe the past that you're ashamed of is what God wants to use to impact the lives of many you come into contact with.

According to verse 12, we have boldness and access with confidence through_____.

Paul reminds us that our boldness and access to God comes through faith. I want you to pause and recognize why this is significant. In the past, Paul thought access to God came through the law. But at Damascus, Jesus showed Paul that this is only through faith in him.

Read Galatians 2:16, Romans 3:20, and Romans 7:6

Unfortunately, there's a works based "gospel" going around and it tries to get people to think that they can earn their way into the presence of God. If they just prayed hard enough, gave enough tithes, or read their Bible long enough, they'd be okay. But that's not true. This comes through faith in Jesus alone.

Prayer for spiritual strength

Read and paraphrase verses 14-19

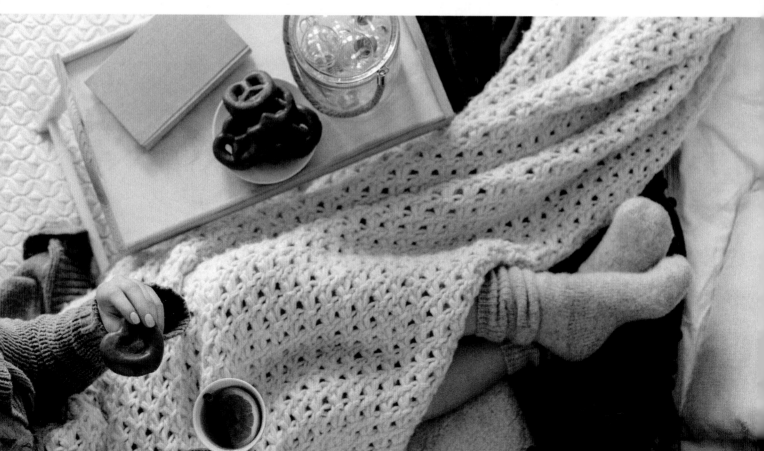

Think about the posture Paul is describing here. Bowing down signifies humility and surrender. Paul is expressing how deeply he needs the Father to fulfill his request. He cares so much about the Ephesians that instead of bowing before God to ask for help with his own personal needs, he prays fervently for them.

God has called you to reach people too. Do you know who they are? Are you praying fervently for them?

What was Paul praying for the Ephesians? List the points he makes.

_____
_____
_____
_____
_____
_____
_____

Why do you think Paul prayed that their love of Christ would surpass knowledge? (also see Revelation 2:1-7)

_____
_____
_____
_____
_____
_____
_____

Read verses 20-21

Doxology

The last few verses of this chapter are known as a doxology.

Here is what CompellingTruth.org says about doxologies:

The word "doxology" literally means a study of praise. However, dictionaries usually define the term as expressions of praise to God, often associated with a hymn sung during Christian worship.

Throughout history, certain songs have been specifically labeled as doxologies by the church. The Catholic Church has primarily used the Gloria Patri or "Great Doxology." There is also a "Lesser Doxology" whose lyrics include, "Glory be to the Father, and to the Son, and to the Holy Ghost. As it was in the beginning, is now and ever shall be, world without end. Amen."

A few other doxologies are found in Jude 1:24-25, Hebrews 13:20-21, and Romans 16:25-27

Paul prayed fervently for the Ephesians but he also recognized that God was able to do much more than he could ask or think and was working within Paul to accomplish his will.

What do you learn about God from these two verses?

_____

_____

_____

_____

_____

_____

_____

_____

Consider memorizing Ephesians 3:20-21

Now to him who is able to do far more abundantly than all that we ask or think, according to the power at work within us, to him be glory in the church and in Christ Jesus throughout all generations, forever and ever. Amen.

Tips for memorizing scripture:

- Write it out word for word 3-5 times
- Listen to the passage using YouVersion's audio feature
- Ask a friend to listen as you repeat the scripture back to him or her
- Use key words and phrases to help you remember
- Create a song or acronym

Start by writing out Ephesians 3:20-21 a few times here and try to complete one or more items from the rest of the list throughout the this week.

Day 2: Living a life worthy of our identity in Christ

Read Ephesians 4:1-32

How does Paul encourage the Ephesians to walk? List the specific words he uses.

_____
_____
_____
_____
_____
_____

What do you think it means to "bear with one another in love?"

_____
_____
_____
_____
_____
_____
_____

What are the gifts Christ gave to men when he ascended?

_____
_____
_____
_____
_____
_____

Why did he give us these gifts?

_____
_____
_____
_____
_____
_____

How do the gentiles walk?

_____
_____
_____
_____
_____
_____

What are some of the consequences of a hardened heart?

_____
_____
_____
_____
_____
_____

Living a life worthy of our identity in Christ

Read verses 1-7

Paul encourages the Ephesians to walk in a manner worthy of their calling. It's great to know how amazing our identity in Christ is but we should also recognize that our identity goes beyond knowledge.

Notice that this is the second time Paul refers to himself as a prisoner of Christ. He thought this calling was so important that he was willing to be put in prison for it. We should treat our calling in Christ the same way and choose to walk worthy of it.

This doesn't mean it will be easy. In fact, this is why Paul will later explain exactly _how_ we can walk worthy of this calling.

How do you walk worthy of your calling in Christ in the everyday?

_____
_____
_____
_____
_____
_____
_____

Paul gives us five things to think about.

1. Humility
2. Gentleness
3. Patience
4. Bearing with one another in love,
5. Eager to maintain the unity of the Spirit in the bond of peace

Humility

Your translation may use the word "lowliness" in place of the word "humility." In the Greek world, humility and lowliness had a very negative association tied to it. No one wanted to be lowly. It meant something was wrong with you. But for Christians, lowliness is a great virtue.

> *True humility is not thinking less of yourself; it is thinking of yourself less.* - C.S. Lewis

Humility doesn't mean that we think less of ourselves. Paul didn't take half of this letter to tell us about our glorious identity in Christ so that we can turn around and think badly of ourselves. Instead, we should be thinking of ourselves less.

How have you always thought of humility? Is it consistent with its true meaning?

_____

_____

_____

_____

_____

_____

_____

In what ways do you struggle to be humble?

_____

_____

_____

_____

_____

_____

Why do you think humility is necessary for a person walking worthy of their calling?

_____

_____

_____

_____

_____

_____

_____

_____

_____

_____

_____

Gentleness

Next, Paul tells us that we should be gentle. The dictionary defines gentleness as a mildness of disposition or meekness. Gentleness is simply treating others with respect and submitting our strength and our rights for the sake of Christ and love towards others.

Did you know that Jesus was often described as gentle and lowly? It's fascinating because he didn't need to be either of those things. He was literally God in the flesh. But he chose to walk in humility and gentleness. If our Savior lived this way, shouldn't we do the same?

Our world looks down on people who are gentle. We're told to be bold, loud, and strong. But what if true strength looks like knowing when to lay down our strength for the sake of others?

Do you struggle with being gentle?

_____
_____
_____
_____
_____
_____
_____

What would gentleness look like in the day to day of your life?

_____
_____
_____
_____
_____
_____
_____

Why is gentleness important for a Christian walking worthy of their calling?

_____
_____
_____
_____
_____
_____
_____
_____
_____
_____
_____

Patience & Bearing with one another in love

We're going to look at these two together because they go hand in hand.

People will do us wrong in many ways. But we should still show them grace and forgiveness since Jesus has done the same for us. Jesus has been so patient with us. We should be patient with others.

Read Matthew 18:21-35

What stands out to you from this passage?

_____
_____
_____
_____
_____
_____
_____
_____
_____
_____

The servant pleaded with his master to forgive his debts and he did. Yet, another servant who owed him way less than he owed his master asked for forgiveness, and he refused to show mercy.

Sometimes we act a lot like the unforgiving servant. We forget the enormous debt God canceled for us and we fail to have mercy on others.

Yes, people may annoy us or even hurt us -- but just as we have been forgiven by God, we should forgive our brother and sisters in Christ.

Do you find it difficult to be patient with your peers? Why or why not?

_____
_____
_____
_____
_____
_____
_____

Think about one person you haven't been so patient with. How can you show them grace this week?

_____
_____
_____
_____
_____
_____

Why do you think choosing patience is important as we walk worthy of our calling?

_____

_____

_____

_____

_____

_____

_____

_____

_____

Eager to maintain the unity of the Spirit

Finally, as we walk out our calling, we should make every effort to maintain the unity of the Spirit in the bond of peace. Notice that Paul used the word "maintain" here. We maintain the unity of the Spirit while recognizing that it was a gift from God.

Why do you think it's necessary to maintain the unity of the Spirit?

_____

_____

_____

_____

_____

_____

_____

_____

_____

What are some of the things that can threaten our unity with fellow believers?

_____

_____

_____

_____

_____

_____

_____

_____

_____

_____

Paul actually goes on to speak even more about unity. In verses 4 through 6 he says, "there is one body and one Spirit... one hope that belongs to your call... one God and father of all..."

The word "one" is repeated here seven times! So, we must recognize that being one is important as believers.

We are all one body of believers and we have been saved by the same Spirit. We all look forward to the same hope. Our one Lord is Jesus Christ and our faith is the same. We have all been baptized into the same body. We worship one God who is the Father of all.

Essentially, we have the same goal. We are all different but our goal and purpose is one.

Paul encourages believers to maintain their unity because this is what the enemy is after. The body is stronger as we all stand together. However, we are weak when we are divided. (See Mark 3:25)

Of the five things Paul gives us to focus on, which do you struggle with most? Once you have identified it, take a moment to express it to God and ask him for help in the area you struggle with.

Day 3: Spiritual Gifts

Read Ephesian 4:7-10

Verse 7 speaks about how God has given us grace according to the measure of Christ's gift.

What do you think this means? (Hint: use the surrounding verses to help you.)

_____

_____

_____

_____

_____

_____

Read 1 Corinthians 12:4-6

God has made us all unique and has empowered each of us to do different things. But everything we do is by the same Spirit for the same purpose.

Fill in the blank.

Variety of gifts → same _____.

Varieties of service → same _____.

Varieties of activities → same _____ who empowers them all in everyone.

When we use our gifts from God, we must recognize that they come from him not from us. We do not boast in our gifts but we don't shy away from them either.

Jesus made a pretty big sacrifice for the gifts we now have. In ancient times, when a king came back from war, he would bring back spoils with him for his people. Jesus went to war and brought back gifts for us. So, we shouldn't take our gifts lightly. He paid a price for them.

Read verses 11-16, Romans 12:6-8, 1 Corinthians 12:7-11, and 1 Corinthians 12:28

List all of the gifts given to the body of Christ:

_____

_____

_____

_____

_____

_____

What is the purpose of the gifts in each of these passages?

_____

_____

_____

_____

_____

_____

I want you to understand that the purpose of these gifts aren't so that we can serve ourselves, they are to glorify God and edify his body. The diversity of the gifts within the body of Christ is meant to promote spiritual unity.

The church needs your gift. Paul goes on to say that spiritual gifts help us in ministry, building up the body, and attaining the unity of the faith. Spiritual gifts also help us to become mature Christians. Each believer is called to "grow up in every way into him who is the head (Christ)." When we are first saved, we are children in the faith. But, we are not meant to remain children. Our faith needs to mature.

All of the spiritual gifts working together actually helps to hold the body together. Without all of us working together, the body will not function properly. If you've ever felt like you or your gifts were not needed, that's not true. You are needed and God is calling you to use your spiritual gifts for the growth of his body. Don't hold back.

Pause & Reflect

What gifts do you feel God has given you?

_____

_____

_____

_____

_____

_____

Do you feel like you're using them to the fullest potential? If not, what's holding you back?

_____

_____

_____

_____

_____

_____

List three ways you can use your spiritual gift(s) this week and make an intentional plan to do so.

_____

_____

_____

_____

_____

_____

Day 4: The New Life in Christ

Read Ephesian 4:17-19

Paul tells us not to walk like the Gentiles do. They walk in the futility of their minds. Earlier we defined futility as "uselessness" or "pointlessness." We have been transformed and called out of that lifestyle so we should live as if we have been changed.

List some of the words Paul uses to describe the Gentiles

_____

_____

_____

_____

_____

Their hardness of heart kept them from understanding the things of God and they were separated from him because of their own ignorance. But, let's pause for a second and recognize that we were once just like this. Jesus' sacrifice on the cross saved us and opened our eyes to the truth.

Since the Gentiles had calloused hearts, they naturally gave themselves over to sensuality and greed. If something is calloused, it has lost sensitivity to touch. A person with a calloused heart has trouble hearing the truth and only God can break down that barrier.

Read Galatians 5:19-24 and complete the rest of the chart:

Works of the flesh	Fruit of the Spirit
Sexual immorality	Love
Impurity	Joy
Sensuality	Peace
Idolatry	Patience
Sorcery	
Enmity	
Strife	

Read verses 20-24

Paul quickly interjects and lets us know that this is not the way we learned in Christ. Sure, we lived like this in the past but now we have learned something new. It's time to put off our old self and our sinful lifestyles and put on our new self and walk in holiness and righteousness.

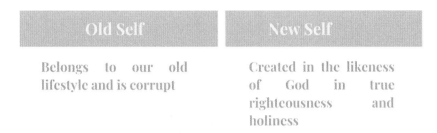

Old Self	New Self
Belongs to our old lifestyle and is corrupt	Created in the likeness of God in true righteousness and holiness

If we have been saved and our lives look no different than it did before we encountered Jesus, something is wrong. The Spirit convicts us of the wrong in our lives and empowers us to change. The question is, are we submitting to the Spirit's work in our lives?

Here are four ways we practically submit to the Spirit:

- We listen for his voice
- We read the word with expectancy
- We pray and confess our sins
- We make an effort to live out what we read in scripture

Previously we spoke about unity and togetherness. Our new life in Christ unites us as believers but separates us from the world. Once we are saved, we make a conscious decision by the help of the Spirit to put away everything in our lives that does not glorify Jesus. This is a day to day process and it doesn't happen all at once. But as the Spirit reveals the things in our lives that need to go, it is our duty to say, "Yes" and surrender everything at his feet.

Think back to chapter 3. We were dead *in* sin but Jesus made us alive in him so that now we are dead *to* sin. There is an obvious distinction between who we once were and who we are now. (See 2 Cor 5:17)

We don't become Christians and add Jesus to our lives. We become Christians and submit to Jesus, allowing him to remove everything that is not like him.

Pause & Reflect

Can you think of anything you may not be submitting to God? If so, confess, repent, and ask him to help you.

_____

_____

_____

_____

_____

_____

_____

_____

Day 5: The New Life in Christ (pt 2)

Read Ephesian 4:25-32

Paul gives us practical instruction here for how we should be living as believers:

- We put away falsehood and speak the truth with one another
- We_____. (see verse 26)
- We give no opportunity for the devil
- We do not steal but instead _____. (see verse 28)
- We do not speak corrupt words but instead _____. (see verse 29)

Notice that Paul encourages us to replace bad habits with good ones. It's not enough to simply stop stealing. Instead, we should begin working with our own hands so that we can provide for ourselves and help others.

Read Matthew 12:43-45

While this speaks specifically about impure spirits, it's applicable here as well. There's no neutrality when it comes to sin. We don't merely turn from evil, we turn towards good.

Have you ever sinned in your anger? What happened?

_____
_____
_____
_____
_____
_____
_____
_____
_____

How do you think we can acknowledge our real feelings of anger without sinning?

_____
_____
_____
_____
_____
_____
_____
_____

Why is it important to do honest work with our own hands instead of taking from others?

_____
_____
_____
_____
_____
_____

What do you think Paul means by "corrupting talk?"

_____
_____
_____
_____
_____
_____
_____
_____

What do you think it means to grieve the Holy Spirit?

_____
_____
_____
_____
_____
_____
_____
_____

How should we not be acting towards each other (see verse 31)?

_____
_____
_____
_____
_____
_____
_____

How should we instead be acting towards each other (see verse 32)?

_____
_____
_____
_____
_____

Our new life in Christ comes with a lot of wonderful benefits. But it also comes with very real responsibility. Though we live in the world, we are from a different kingdom. The beliefs and lifestyle of the world will always try to infiltrate our hearts. We are in a constant battle against sin.

But we overcome by sticking close to the Lord in prayer and by reading his word. It gets hard but we should choose to obey his voice. The good news is, he hasn't left us alone to deal with our sin. He has conquered sin for us at the cross. As we walk into holiness and remove the lifestyle of sin from our hearts, he helps us. God is no longer standing as our judge, he is our Father and he is willing to help us.

If you struggle with sin, do not feel condemned. There is so much hope for you. Bring all of it to God and trust him to help you.

God is our Father & he's willing to help us.

week 4

Practical Holiness

FINALLY, BE STRONG IN THE LORD AND IN THE STRENGTH OF HIS MIGHT.

ephesians 6:10

Day 1: Imitators of God

Read Ephesians 5:1-33 and 6:1-24

Make note of important keywords, phrases, and anything else that stands out to you.

_____
_____
_____
_____
_____
_____
_____
_____
_____
_____
_____
_____
_____
_____

Now read verses 1 and 2

Notice that chapter five opens up with the word "therefore." Paul is going to introduce key things about how we should live in light of our new life in Christ.

What are two things Paul encourages us to do?

_____
_____
_____
_____

He tells us to be imitators of God as beloved children and to walk in love as Christ has loved us.

In many cases, it's not good to be a follower. But in this case, we are called to be followers of God as children follow their parents. Think about it. Children love and trust their parents and they believe that their parents have their best interests in mind. Likewise, we follow God believing that he has our best interests in mind. Even when we don't understand where he's leading us, we choose to follow him anyway.

Do you think it's a hard task to be an imitator of God? Why or why not?

_____
_____
_____
_____
_____
_____

If you answered yes, I totally get it. But the beautiful thing about this phrase is that it's not telling us to be *perfect* imitators of God and it doesn't imply that we're doing this on our own. I don't know about you but I've never seen a child imitate their parent perfectly. They usually mess up over and over again. But, as they grow older, they get better. Their parents are with them helping them along the way. This is how we imitate God. We trust him to help us and we remember that he's with us guiding us along the way and wants us to succeed.

Next, Paul tells us to walk in love as Christ loved us. Christ is our example: he loved us and literally sacrificed his life for us. Because of his love for us, we can love God and each other.

These two phrases anchor this entire section of scripture. In a bit, we'll discuss a lot of things we shouldn't be doing. It's important to know and avoid those things. But if we want to effectively avoid the things we shouldn't be doing, we should focus on what we should do. Paul gives us the formula from the very beginning. Be imitators of God and walk in love.

That being said, let's dive into discussing practical holiness.

Read verses 3-6

List the sins Paul points out:

_____

_____

_____

_____

Which three sins does Paul say shouldn't even be named among believers?

_____

_____

_____

_____

Before we jump into discussing these sins, I want to share something from David Guzik:

> We must notice the theme of the moral appeal. It isn't "avoid these things so that you can be a saint." Rather, it is "you are a saint; now live in a manner fitting for a saint." The constant moral appeal of the New Testament is simply this: be who you are in Jesus. - David Guzik

As we look at these sins, we must remember that Jesus has won the victory over them. He's walking with us as we seek to remove them from our lives.

The emphasis on this chapter is sexual sin. The city of Ephesus especially struggled with this sin. Remember that the Ephesians worshiped the goddess Diana. The cult of Diana included ritual prostitution that required the worshiper to be joined with the goddess through her priestess. Idolatry and sexual sin were very much intertwined in Ephesus.

Ephesus was in many ways similar to our culture today. We live in a culture that is morally bankrupt and all of the things considered holy by God are twisted and profaned. This is an emphatic wakeup call from Paul to the Ephesian Christians not to continue following the lifestyle that their neighbors indulged in.

Read John 17:14-19

It can be disheartening to know that everything around us is promoting sin and ungodliness. It's hard to resist the temptation of the world. But here in John 17, we see that Jesus prays to the Father to keep his people safe because while they live in the world, they are not of the world.

Life will get hard and temptation will come. John reminds us that Jesus is our advocate when we sin. We can go to Jesus, confess, and find help when we are in need. (See 1 John 2:1)

So, if you struggle with any of these sins know that there is no condemnation. All your sins have been forgiven in Christ and by God's grace you can overcome.

Sexual Immorality

Sexual immorality includes all sexual sin. Sexual immorality is any sexual thought or action that is outside of God's design for human sexuality.

Our culture has a problem. We point out certain sexual sins as wrong while ignoring others. For example, we recognize that sexual intercourse before marriage is a sin but we don't think of our secret lust filled thoughts as sinful. If we want victory over sexual sin, we must be willing to allow God to cleanse us of all perverted sexuality in our lives.

Impurity

Impurity refers to any kind of unclean thoughts or lifestyles. Again, God wants us to be free from impure and unclean thoughts as much as he wants us to be free from physical sexual acts.

Covetousness

Covetousness is a lustful desire for something that belongs to someone else. In this context, Paul is specifically speaking about the desire for someone else's spouse.

This brings us back to the tenth commandment in Exodus 20.

Why do you think covetousness is such a problem?

_____

_____

_____

_____

_____

_____

Covetousness is discontentment with what God has given us. The discontentment in our hearts can lead to other sinful thoughts and actions. Instead of desiring what belongs to another, we should be thankful for the gifts God has given us.

Filthiness, foolish talk and crude joking

Again, in this context, Paul was most likely referring to sexual innuendos. Context is really important here. Paul isn't condemning joking, he's condemning sinful forms of joking that dishonor God and each other.

While we should obviously be avoiding physical sexual sin and impure lifestyles, it is also important to make sure that our speech aligns with who we are in Christ. If we value God's holy design for sexuality, why would we be speaking about it in a way that perverts God's design?

Let's not only examine our actions. May we also examine our hearts, our thoughts, motives, and our speech. If we have been transformed and are now children of God, we must live it out.

Foolish and crude joking may seem innocent but it actually damages us and other believers.

Paul tells us that instead of foolish talk and crude joking, our mouths should be filled with thanksgiving.

Not only are these sins serious, Paul also says that people who practice these things have no inheritance in the kingdom of God. Now, he's not saying that if we struggle with these things we won't inherit the kingdom. If we are true believers, our hearts will be convicted about these things.

Even if we say we are Christians and still habitually practice these things without submitting them to God, we're actually deceiving ourselves. Our identity in Christ is also evident in the way we live.

If we have been transformed, we must live it out.

Pause & Reflect

Today's study was pretty heavy and we talked about a lot of sin. I want you to remember that as a believer, there is no condemnation. If we confess our sins, God is faithful to forgive us. So, I want you to reflect in prayer. What sins do you struggle with? Tell them to God and ask for his help in removing them from your life.

_____
_____
_____
_____
_____
_____
_____
_____
_____
_____
_____
_____
_____
_____
_____
_____
_____
_____
_____
_____

Day 2: Separate from the world

Read Ephesians 5:8-14

Fill in the blank.

> Therefore do not become _____ with them; for at one time you were _____, but now you are _____ in the Lord. Walk as children of light (for the fruit of light is found in all that is good and right and true), and try to _____ what is pleasing to the Lord. Take _____ in the unfruitful works of darkness, but instead _____ them.

Describe what it means to be a "partner" with someone else.

_____

_____

_____

_____

Partnering with someone means that you are participating in the same things they participate in. When Paul says do not be partners with them, he doesn't mean that you can't be friends or acquaintances with people who practice these things. He does mean that our lives shouldn't be wrapped up and intertwined with theirs. There should be a clear distinction between who you are and what you stand for and who they are and what they stand for.

Read Luke 14:25-33

Jesus tells the crowd following him that if they are not willing to forsake everything to follow him, they cannot be his disciple. The point of Jesus' words is not that we should go around hating people or even ourselves. But if our family and friends and even our own personal desires keep us from obeying God, we should be willing to let them go. There is a real cost to discipleship. We have to let go of the things that do not honor God and cling to the things that do.

Maybe you have family and friends who are living sinful lifestyles. This doesn't mean to reject them or be unkind towards them. But, we simply can't be involved with some of the conversations they have, or the events they go to, or the things they do. We have to be separate.

Once you have seen the light, there is no point going back into the darkness. How can a child of light walk in darkness? It's impossible, right?

Not only are we called to forsake sin, we are also called to expose it. Let us look within our hearts. Can we genuinely say we are separate from sin or do we secretly love it?

So far this chapter might feel like a lot. But Paul isn't telling us to do anything we can't do. If we have been saved, we have also been empowered by the Spirit to walk out our new life in Christ. As believers, the truest and deepest desires of our heart are to honor God. Of course there are distractions in the world but if we stay in God's word, he keeps us safe from those distractions. (See John 15:4)

Walking carefully

Read verses 15-21

The Christian walk is a careful walk. We make wise, spirit-led choices because we know our lives have purpose and meaning. As you try to walk carefully, a good question to ask yourself is,

How does this thought or action glorify God, point the world to Jesus, and edify me and fellow believers?

We must make the most of every God-given opportunity and use it purposefully.

We can walk wisely when we know God's will. It might seem like a hard task but it isn't. If we are faithful to read God's word and pray regularly, we will know his will. Otherwise, we will be easily led astray by things that seem right in our own eyes but are really wrong.

Paul specifically speaks of drunkenness as one way we often walk unwisely. He says instead of being drunk with wine, we should be filled with the Spirit. The Spirit enables us to live righteously but drunkenness removes our inhibitions and instead of being able to make good decisions, we are more susceptible to making poor ones.

The words coming out of our mouth should be pure. We address each other with psalms, hymns and spiritual songs. We constantly overflow with praise and gratitude to God and all he's done for us.

We make wise, spirit-led choices because we know our lives have purpose and meaning.

Day 3: Instructions for our relationships

We're going to discuss the three important types of relationships Paul focuses on in this section. He speaks about relationships between a husband and wife, parents and children, and servants and masters. Let's take a closer look at each of these.

Wives and husbands:

Read Ephesians 5:22-33

Why do you think Paul tells wives to submit to their husbands?

_____
_____
_____
_____
_____
_____
_____

Why do you think Paul tells husbands to love their wives?

_____
_____
_____
_____
_____
_____
_____

I love David Guzik's commentary on these verses:

> *submission does not mean inferiority. It means sub-mission. Putting yourself under a mission. The mission is more important than your individual desires. - David Guzik*

Wives are not putting themselves below their husbands but instead, they are putting themselves below the mission God has for their marriage. **Submission does not imply subservience.**

Jesus actually illustrates a beautiful picture of submission in his own life. He submitted perfectly to the Father's will. Yet, Jesus was completely equal to the Father.

I also want to point out that wives submit to their *own* husbands not to every man. Submission is only applicable in the context of a relationship. Ultimately, wives' motives for submission should come from their love and dedication to Christ.

Likewise, husbands should love their wives as Christ loves the church. That's a huge call. This implies sacrificial love. Husbands should love their wives as they love their own bodies.

This beautiful picture of a Godly relationship also illustrates Christ's relationship with the church.

Parents & Children:

Read Ephesians 5:1-4 and Exodus 20:12

Fill in the blank.

Children are encouraged to obey their parents _____.

The first commandment with a promise was to honor our parents. The Bible often speaks of an important system of honor, submission, and obedience. This does not mean we have no rights or opinions, it just means that in humility, we are willing to submit to someone else.

This system goes against our natural tendency to be prideful. (See James 4:6)

If we refuse to honor and respect each other, it shows a lot about how we honor and respect God. If children cannot respect the authority of their parents, how will they learn to respect God's authority?

Now on the other hand, parents are told not to provoke their children to wrath. Paul knows that we are human and parents can be tempted to disrespect their children. This isn't a one-sided system. We should all be treating each other with grace and respect.

Instead of provoking their children to wrath, parents should be teaching them how to love and honor God.

Let's be real, it's not always easy to honor our parents. Especially as adult children. We may often clash with them. But we can be firm in our identity and still show honor to our parents.

Bondservants & Masters:

Read Ephesians 5:5-9

First, let me just say that the Bible does not condone slavery and ancient Greek slavery was completely different than modern-day slavery. The term "bondservant" covers a wide range of services. Sometimes people volunteered in order to pay off a debt and other times it was a more permanent role of service. Historians actually estimate that in the first century, ⅓ of the Roman population were bondservants.

New Testament writers often referred to themselves as bondservants of Christ. This is significant because they viewed Christ as their permanent master. This wasn't a "job" they could leave, it was a full-time role.

No one wanted to be a bondservant but if this was their role, there was a right and wrong way to live out that role. Sometimes we are stuck in situations we don't want to be in. Faithfulness and obedience to God is important anyway.

How should servants act towards their earthly masters?

_____
_____
_____
_____
_____

We might not be able to relate to this 100% but we can relate in terms of our careers or even school. We won't always love the things that our bosses or our teachers do but we should still honor them as unto the Lord. We should remember that our ultimate reward comes from Christ, not man.

Again, Paul doesn't leave this conversation one-sided. He instructs masters to treat their servants as they would want to be treated.

Maybe you have a leadership role over someone else. Remember that how you treat the people you lead is important. Are you treating them with love and respect? Are you leading with humility?

In each of these occasions, we are all accountable to Christ. Leaders are called to submit to Christ and in submitting to him, we learn to love and lead others well.

Pause & Reflect

Take a moment to think about your personal relationships. How do each of these relationships reflect the gospel? How does your identity in Christ inform how you act within these relationships? What are some things you can do to ensure that these relationships glorify God?

_____
_____
_____
_____
_____
_____
_____
_____
_____
_____
_____
_____
_____
_____
_____
_____
_____
_____
_____
_____
_____
_____
_____
_____
_____
_____
_____
_____

Day 4: Engaging in spiritual warfare

Read Ephesians 6:10-24

Paul encourages us to be strong in _____.

This always stands out to me because it is a reminder that our strength doesn't come from our knowledge, wisdom, or achievements, it comes from the Lord. It is impossible to navigate living in this world without Christ.

Paul isn't calling us to muster up our own strength or pull ourselves up by our bootstraps. Instead, he's calling us to depend on and draw from the strength of the Lord.

We've learned a lot so far about what it means to live a Christian life. If there's one thing we can agree on, it's not easy. We are threatened by the temptations of the world, our own flesh, and the spiritual attacks of Satan. It's hard but remember that Christ has already overcome and he has given us his strength.

How do we become strong in the Lord?

_____
_____
_____
_____
_____
_____
_____
_____

We can also become strong in the Lord by putting on the whole armor of God. We'll take a look at the specific details of the armor in a second but first, let's look at why it's even important to wear this armor.

According to verse 11, why is it important to put on the whole armor of God?

_____
_____
_____
_____
_____
_____
_____

We need to be discerning because although our enemy is real, our enemy is not each other. We are wrestling against something much more sinister here. While we're going to want to direct our energy against people, Paul reminds us not to. Our fight is not against flesh and blood. We must always remember to direct our energy against Satan and his evil schemes.

Read John 10:10

According to this verse, Satan has three main agendas. He wants to steal, kill, and destroy. And the thing is, he'll use anyone and anything he can get to. Don't be surprised if he uses your friends, family, co-workers, and even random people on the internet to try and harm you.

Regardless of what he's using, we must recognize him and resist him.

Read James 4:7

Resisting the devil is not merely trying to avoid him. We resist him by standing firmly against him. We can only do this by God's word and his Spirit working in our hearts.

Whole armor of God

List the key parts of the armor:

_____
_____
_____
_____
_____
_____
_____
_____
_____
_____
_____
_____
_____
_____
_____

Armor	Purpose	Spiritual Meaning
Belt of truth	In a battle, the belt protects the soldier's abdomen and gathers up their long garments to help them fight effectively. Technically, the belt isn't a part of the armor. However, it is its foundation. Without the belt, the soldier couldn't put on the rest of his armor.	God's truth is our foundation. We cannot be successful in this fight without it.
Breastplate of righteousness	A soldier's breastplate protected all of their vital organs.	God's righteousness covers us just as a breastplate covered Roman soldiers. Put on the righteousness of Christ that he died to give you. You cannot fight with your own righteousness, you need the Lord's. (See Isaiah 64:6)
Protective shoes	Soldiers wore protective sandals to cover their feet in battle.	The gospel of peace should be our "protective shoes" in battle against the enemy. It is our foundation and everything we do springs from it.

Armor	Purpose	Spiritual Meaning
Shield of faith	Fiery darts were used to attack opponents in warfare. The soldier used their shield to deflect these darts.	The enemy is going to use many things to attack us. We must use our faith to throw those darts back at him so they do not harm us.
Helmet of salvation	The helmet protected the soldier's head, an essential part of the body.	Likewise, the truth about our salvation protects us spiritually. Our salvation is secure and no one can take it away from us.
The sword of the spirit	Finally, a soldier always carried a sword with them. It was their offensive weapon.	The sword of the Spirit is the word of God. (Also see Hebrews 4:12)

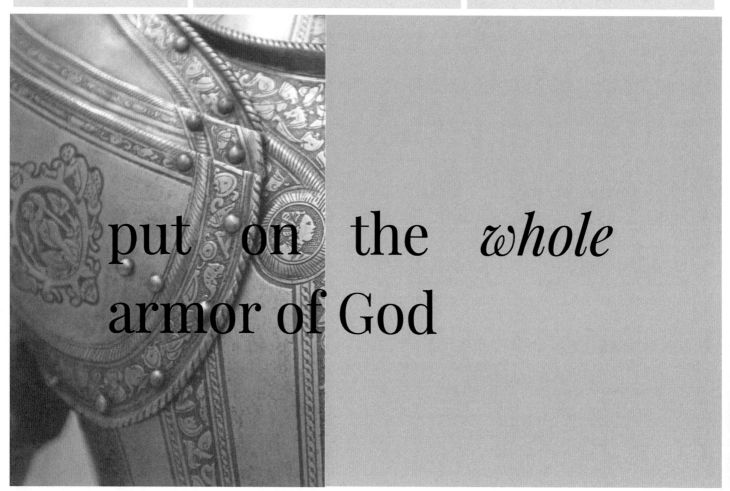

put on the *whole* armor of God

Why do you think it's important to know God's truth in today's world?

_____

_____

_____

_____

_____

_____

_____

What do you think some of the challenges might be for a believer who does not have a foundation of truth?

_____

_____

_____

_____

_____

_____

_____

Do you ever feel tempted to rely on your own righteousness? How can you remind yourself to rely on God's righteousness instead?

_____

_____

_____

_____

_____

_____

_____

Why do you think the gospel of peace is represented as protective shoes?

_____

_____

_____

_____

_____

_____

_____

What fiery darts have the enemy been throwing at you lately?

_____

_____

_____

_____

_____

_____

List four ways you can strengthen your faith to resist these darts.

_____
_____
_____
_____
_____
_____
_____

Do you ever struggle with believing that your salvation is secure? Why or why not?

_____
_____
_____
_____
_____
_____
_____

The sword of the Spirit is the word of God. Do you feel confident in using the word in spiritual warfare?

_____
_____
_____
_____
_____
_____
_____

Praying in the spirit

Next, Paul encourages us to pray in the Spirit.

Read James 5:13-18

Spiritual warfare is HARD. This is why we need to present everything to God in prayer and supplication. We often make the mistake of trying to fight these battles on our own. When we do, we won't be able to overcome it. But if we seek the Lord in this battle, we will be victorious.

Be alert, persevere, pray for each other

All of us are in spiritual warfare whether we know it or not. We need each other's strength. We pray for each other so that God would help us endure to the end.

There is so much beauty to our identity in Christ. But this identity also comes with hardship and battles. Christ has already overcome. Remember that. Use the word as your weapon against the enemy and as your guide for living a righteous life. Walk by the Spirit and allow him to lead you into all truth. God is with us and we have each other. We are never alone.

Closing & Summary

Congratulations! You've made it to the end of our study of Ephesians. I hope you enjoyed this study and I hope you learned a lot. Before we part ways, let's wrap up some of the key points we discussed.

- God has given us spiritual blessings as a part of our inheritance in Christ
- We have been predestined by God to be holy and blameless before him
- No one can take away our salvation. We are sealed by the Holy Spirit.
- We were dead in trespasses and sin but Christ made us alive by dying on the cross for our sins.
- Our salvation is by grace through faith. It's nothing we could earn.
- We put away our old life and put on our new life when we are in Christ
- There are practical standards of holiness that we should live by
- Spiritual warfare is real but God has given us all the weapons we need to fight

Final Reflection

What stood out to you most about this study?

_____
_____
_____
_____
_____
_____
_____

What are some things that were challenging to believe?

_____
_____
_____
_____
_____
_____
_____

What do you feel you need to be praying for?

_____
_____
_____
_____
_____
_____
_____
_____
_____
_____

How will your Christian walk be different after completing this study?

_____

_____

_____

_____

_____

_____

_____

_____

_____

If you feel comfortable sharing, I'd love to hear how this study impacted you. Please email me your thoughts at shante@herstyleoftea.com. Only email anything you are comfortable sharing publicly as your testimony may be shared.

Thank you for joining me for this study!

References:

1. Map of Asia Minor: ESV.org
2. Map of Paul's Third Missionary Journey: Apostle Paul's Third Journey Large Map
3. Key Themes of Ephesians Paraphrased Introduction to Ephesians
4. Ligioner Ministries: Predestination: How Does It Reveal the Glory of God?
5. The Ground is Even at the Foot of the Cross - Blake Guichet
6. Definition of "Boasting" from the Oxford Dictionary
7. John Piper on Boasting: Justification by Faith Is the End of Boasting
8. Wall of Hostility: Topical Bible: Court of the Gentiles
9. Photo of Temple Court During Herod's Rule: Virtual Model of the Temple Mount in the Time of Jesus
10. Your ministry is found quote... (unknown)
11. Doxologies: What is a doxology, and is it found in the Bible?
12. True Humility Quote: Rick Warren, The Purpose Driven Life: What on Earth Am I Here for?
13. David Guzik on Saints: Ephesians Chapter 5
14. Cult of Diana: Cult Prostitution In New Testament Ephesus: A Reappraisal by SM Baugh
15. David Guzik on Submission: Ephesians Chapter 5